Thinking Deficit Disorder

By: Rich Decabo

Thinking
Deficit
Disorder

Rich Decabo

*A **stupid man's** report of what a
clever **man** says can never be accurate,*

Although Thinking Deficit Disorder is not a clinical term, I have created it as a philosophical phrase to refer to people who do not spend much time on thinking about general things.
General things may sound harmless but there are consequences to those poor or lack of, thinking habits.

If people believe in misconceptions, again, perhaps not especially important, but yet, wrongly believed in, how do people perceive larger issues?

If the reasons are the same, that being, lack of time and energy put into thinking, then false or distorted beliefs can lead to more significant consequences raging from arguments to disputes and even physical violence.
Even the power of the vote can be a major problem because of the years of consequences that may lay ahead.

Why does the average person believe that blood is blue inside the body and turns red when it is exposed to oxygen?

Why do so many people believe that sugar makes children hyper?

Blood is red inside and outside of the body and there is no evidence whatsoever that a lot of sugar causes a sugar rush or causes children to be hyperactive.

At least, when someone believes that
peenies are made out of copper. They are
not all together wrong.
They would be right if they had forty-year-
old pennies in their pocket.
But for the last forty years, pennies are made
out of zinc.
Ironically, quarters and dimes are made out
of copper!

I was not the smartest student in school, but
when I was in high school, people still
asked, 'If a tree fell in a forest and no one
was around to hear it, did it make a noise?'

Even at that stage in my life where I was
quite naïve and ignorant, it didn't make
sense to me that sounds couldn't exist if
people were not present to hear them.

That misconception, however, has more to
do with most people's self-centeredness than
misguided thoughts.
Although, lack of thinking time does
contribute to that example as well.

A man named Dr. Norman Webb came up with an organizational chart of human thinking.
It is called the **Webb's depth of knowledge chart.**

The chart is a derivative of the more famous and older, Bloom's taxonomy.

Both charts are quite similar.

Webb's Depth of Knowledge chart is broken into four levels of thinking, ranging from common and/or simple forms of intelligence which are represented by words under the category 1on the circle to the highest form and/or uncommon forms of intelligence which are represented by words under the category 4.

According to the chart, people who mostly and/or only use skills such as recall (memorized material) are very common and is one of the lowest forms of intelligence. Ironically, many people respect that level. Perhaps because they do not know any better or are not of the higher forms of thinking.
Most people are impressed by an individual if they "know" a lot of words or topics or facts.
However, according to both Bloom and Webb, it is not a special form of intelligence and they go so far as to deem them, poor or low forms of intelligence.

A couple of examples of level 4 intelligence is creativity and judgement.

Many people understand that creativity is not very common but they have are more difficult time believing and understanding how judgment can be considered a higher form of intelligence.

Perhaps that is because many people may confuse judgement and opinion.
Because anyone can have an opinion may mean that anyone can judge something.

It is true, however, again, people do not often think that opinions can vary in quality.
Many people think that anyone is entitled to an opinion so no one is "right", therefore, no one's opinion is "better" than anyone else's.
Well, that is a fallacy.
How?
If you have a certain pain in an area of your body, who's opinion would you take, an ice cream vendor or a doctor?
A doctor gives you their opinion.

An expert of a given area has an opinion on a matter pertaining to that area of expertise.
A person with little or no knowledge in that area has opinion about the same matter.
Do you take them both at equal value?
I am not suggesting that you do not listen to both or automatically assume that the layman is wrong.

However, it is important that you understand that people who study, learn and know about an area are most likely to be closer to the truth or at least more accurate than a person who barley knows about the area.

I of course, am not referring to a flavor of ice cream.
Chocolate can not be better than vanilla.
That is up to individual preference.
The same for a movie.
However, with a movie, anyone can like a movie but if one wants to discuss which movie had more skilled acting or better production, then opinions can be finer tuned. But since movies are for entertainment, one can enjoy a poorly produced film or one that didn't have quality acting or intelligent script.

All I would ask for is that one respects the opinion of a person who pays attention to the production of a movie and has learned about them and has spent time comparing productions and levels of acting as well as people who have studied film.

I would like to go back to Webb's chart because forms of intelligence are not just, simple opinions.

Almost everyone can agree that creativity is not common.

Perhaps people do not think judging or critiquing is a high form of intelligence, but then again, when one is confronted by someone who judges something, they usually think of it along the lines of that person expressing his or her opinion.

And that is where certain problems arise.

When I am having a discussion with an individual or small group of individuals, I always stress the importance of facts or at least, backing evidence.
If I provide facts and or evidence, I expect the other person to do the same,
If they do not, then I try to keep the discussion or argument to a very limited time frame because emotions can easily

become involved and then one is no longer discussing a topic but fighting.

Another higher order thinking skill is **Synthesis** in the level 3 domain.

That term refers to someone taking two or more pieces of information and combining them to achieve a new idea or better understanding of a known thought or topic.
For example,
All mammals are warm blooded and give birth to live babies.
A bird lays eggs.
A snake is cold blooded.
Neither of them therefore, are not mammals.
On the opposite side,
A bear is warm blooded and gives birth to live babies.
Therefore, a bear is a mammal.

Yes, it is true that those are rather simple forms of synthesizing, but it is important to know what the skill entails.
Synthesis can be applied to any idea or topic.

Although, when it becomes social-political, people tend to stop thinking about it too much.

Emotions are a major cause of Thinking Deficit Disorder.

When I said, earlier, that a person's lack of thinking habits can lead to conflicts, it is because people do not like being wrong, but they don't make more of an effort to be more correct.
Emotions can vary and have positive impacts on an individual's perception and negative impacts.

By positive, I mean that emotions can enhance one's views by motivating thought. For example, perhaps creativity is something one is born with or something that can be developed over time.
In either case, it takes a lot of passion and desire to create. Those emotions behind that desire are positive.

The negative emotions such as jealousy and greed most of the time, lead to counterproductive and even destructive consequences.

The way to achieve the balance between feeling and thinking clearly is governing those emotions.
Not suppressing them or burying them, but to combine them with thought.
It is a difficult procedure, and many people give up or do not bother to govern their emotions.
I believe that the reason most people do not control their emotions is because they wither do not know how or do not believe it is possible.

It is not only possible but quite probable as long as one is persistent and somewhat consistently disciplined.

What one needs to keep in mind is that if one does not govern their emotions in time, those very emotions can begin to distort a person's thoughts.

People are aware that they can be logical
and efficient in things and then when it
comes to other things, they seem to have
difficulty behaving rationally or logically.
Why?
Emotions.
Especially, ungoverned emotions.

All one has to do is think about the
thousands and thousands of people that have
murdered their spouse, parent or best friend
over money.

Their logical mind was overtaken by greed
and they were caught by the police because
they did not think their plan through.
Many thought they did, but their thoughts
were diluted by emotions.

Emotions are not the only inhibitor of
logical thinking.
There are other disabling components in the
mind.

Obviously, there are people who simply
have lower IQ levels, so they are mentally
limited.

However, there is another negative dynamic which causes people to not think correctly, clearly, or logically.

It is the detrimental lack of empathy that I refer to.

Empathy is different than sympathy and quite a number of people, often confuse the two or believe that they mean the same thing.

Sympathy is when one feels sorry for another. When one shows pity for another.

Empathy is when one attempts to put themselves into the mental, emotional and/or physical state of another.

Many people are sympathetic, but few people are empathetic.

I will discuss empathy and the lack of it, later in the book.

I would like to start with other forms of Thinking Deficit Disorders.

First, I will return to synthesis.
The following example will demonstrate how the lack of synthesis can be literally, dangerous.

This example, fortunately, only shows how close the lack of synthesis came to being an utter disaster for tens of millions of people.

In 1936, Adolf Hitler began to build up his military.
He was not supposed to according to the treaty at the end of World War 1, but Europe allowed him to break the rules and increase the size of Germany's military way beyond the amount he was limited to by contract.

By 1938, Hitler had one of the largest armed forces on the planet.
Again, he was allowed to because no one wanted to interfere and start another war.
But was there much logical thought involved in the complacent countries around Germany?

None, at all.
The other European countries hoped that Hitler wanted a powerful military only to protect his country.
And even though Hitler's rhetoric gave apparent signs of expansion beyond his borders, they still hoped that he would not invade anyone.

They could have prevented Germany's built up legally but chose not to.

They only, continued to hope and wait to see that Hitler would only use his army for defense.

The following year, Germany invaded Poland on September 1st, 1939.

England and France declared war on Germany.

So, instead of losing a few thousand soldiers by attacking Germany in 1936, they lost one hundred thousand soldiers.

But as horrible as that was, it became much,
much worse.

The United States sat by and allowed the
war to grow in Europe.
And it was not the government's fault.
The public did not want to attack Germany
and end the war early.

Why?
Because they did not think about it clearly.
Because they did not synthesis.
Because they had Thinking Deficit Disorder.

Nazi Germany quickly defeated Poland,
dividing the country with the Soviet Union,
which had invaded Poland from the east.
Hitler proposed a truce, vowing that millions
would die if Great Britain and France
refused to agree to Germany's demands.

Q   If it appears that Germany is defeating
England and France, should -the United
States declare war
Gallup, Oct. 5-10, 1939
29% said yes and 71% said NO

The United States President, Franklin
Roosevelt and his congress did not want to
declare war when over 70% of his country
did not want to go to war.

The German Army invaded the Netherlands,
Belgium, and France.
Q   Do you think the United States should
declare war on Germany and send our army
and navy abroad to fight?
Gallup, May 18-23, 1940
7% said yes and 93% said NO

Even after Germany invaded several
countries after Poland, instead of realizing

Hitler's goal which was to dominate the world, the public not only remained the same but rejected getting involved and stopping Germany early, even more!
Only 7% wanted to end the war and over 90% didn't!

Nazi Germany defeated France within six weeks, despite the fact that France had mobilized five million men to fight. When France surrendered, the country was divided into Nazi-occupied territory in the north and Nazi-allied territory in the south.
Great Britain became the only major power at war with Nazi Germany and its collaborators.
Q   Which of these two things do you think is the more important for the United States to try to do–to keep out of war ourselves or to help England win, even at the risk of getting into the war?
Gallup, June 27-July 3, 1940
35% said Help 61% said KEEP OUT

France surrendered to Germany as did other countries and Germany showed no signs of slowing down.
The public slowly began to realize what Hitler was up to a year later.
Now 35% wanted to go to war and keep it in Europe before it spread.
But more than 60% still wanted to keep out of the war.

The Japanese attack on the US naval base in Pearl Harbor, Hawaii, led President Franklin Roosevelt to declare war on Japan. A few days later, Nazi Germany declared war on the United States, and America entered World War II against the Axis powers.
Q Should President Roosevelt have declared war on Germany, as well as on Japan?
Gallup, Dec. 12-17, 1941
91% said Yes and 7% said No

It took our nation to be attacked before the public finally agreed that stopping Hitler and Japan was necessary, more than two years began Hitler invaded Poland.

After that, Hitler invaded Russia, so the proof of capturing the world was even more obvious.

If people used the thought process of synthesis, they would have realized Hitler's intention much earlier and save millions of lives.

But instead, the United States attacked Germany almost three years after the first invasion.

Y2K

Why did so many people become hysterical over the upcoming year in 1999?

People's lack of thinking.
Just when they questioned whether or not a tree made a sound when it hit the ground if no one was there to hear it.

Instead of doing a little research into what the changing of the millennia
meant, most people only listened to gossip and exaggerated stories.

People should have spent just a little time and a little energy so determine if changing the dates on computers would have an effect at all.
But their lack of understanding by their own choice, of an approaching event caused people to wastefully worry over it.

The Y2K bug was a computer flaw, or bug, that may have caused problems when dealing with dates beyond December 31, 1999. The flaw, faced by computer programmers and users all over the world on January 1, 2000, is also known as the "millennium bug." (The letter K, which stands for kilo (a unit of 1000), is commonly used to represent the number 1,000. So, Y2K stands for Year 2000.) Many skeptics believe it was barely a problem at all.

When complicated computer programs were being written during the 1960s through the 1980s, computer engineers used a two-digit

code for the year. The "19" was left out.
Instead of a date reading 1970, it read 70.
Engineers shortened the date because data
storage in computers was costly and took up
a lot of space.

As the year 2000 approached, computer
programmers realized that computers might
not interpret 00 as 2000, but as 1900.
Activities that were programmed on a daily
or yearly basis would be damaged or flawed.
As December 31, 1999, turned into January
1, 2000, computers might interpret
December 31, 1999, turning into January 1,
1900.

Banks, which calculate interest rates on a
daily basis, faced real problems. Interest
rates are the amount of money a lender, such
as a bank, charges a customer, such as an
individual or business, for a loan. Instead of
the rate of interest for one day, the computer
would calculate a rate of interest
for *minus* almost 100 years!

Centers of technology, such as power plants,
were also threatened by the Y2K bug. Power

plants depend on routine computer maintenance for safety checks, such as water pressure or radiation levels. Not having the correct date would throw off these calculations and possibly put nearby residents at risk.

Transportation also depends on the correct time and date. Airlines in particular were put at risk, as computers with records of all scheduled flights would be threatened after all, there were very few airline flights in 1900.

Y2K was both
a software and hardware problem. Software refers to the electronic programs used to tell the computer what to do. Hardware is the machinery of the computer itself. Software and hardware companies raced to fix the bug and provided "Y2K compliant" programs to help. The simplest solution was the best: The date was simply expanded to a four-digit number. Governments, especially

in the United States and the United Kingdom, worked to address the problem.

The fallout shelter was ready. The batteries were in place, candles were prepped, food was stocked and the sauced had been jarred — as my grandma prepped for impending doom.

Fear gripped my then-66-year-old grandmother as she tuned into the news and saw what could bring catastrophe to civilization. She urged her children and grandchildren to shelter in place with her as the minutes to midnight rapidly approached.

I am-a gonna be ready for the 2-2-K!"

In her Italian-accented English, that was the mantra of my Sicilian grandma in the months, weeks, days and hours leading up to the turn of the 21st century. Though our family got a good laugh out of her mispronunciation of the Y2K moniker, short for Year 2000, the panic for her and so many people around the globe about what could happen when the clock struck midnight on Jan. 1, 2000, was no laughing matter.

In 1999, Y2K was shorthand for a computer bug that many believed would break the world's electronic systems. They were convinced the bug would prevent online clocks from turning forward to 2000, instead turning them back to 1900 — and cause banks, electrical grids, nuclear power stations and anything driven by a computer to fail.

Y2K was introduced into the mainstream lexicon in the late 1990s, as experts weighed in on the potential likelihood of a digital pandemic. The bigger picture was clear, but the details weren't as easy to grasp.

"There wasn't a very clear explanation of what might actually happen," Alexander George, editor-in-chief of *Popular Mechanics*, told InsideEdition.com. " It stemmed from this basic idea that if the date information is incorrect, that's going to have lots of unintended consequences."

"You had friends who were building safe spaces for nuclear fallout in their backyards. They were stockpiling rations, they were stockpiling water," George explained. "You heard about grocery stores ... running out. I never went through that. But you knew other families that did it.

"Building up to it, you heard stories about runs on ATMs," George continued. "But in general, what you saw, it was preparation for this thing you see in the movies, where money doesn't matter anymore, it's all your survival."

Ghosts

Why do people believe in ghosts?

Is it a rational belief or an emotional belief?

Places that are haunted are usually believed to be associated with some occurrence or emotion in the ghost's past; they are often a former home or the place where he or she died. Aside from actual ghostly apparitions, traditional signs of haunting range from strange noises, lights, odors or breezes to the displacement of objects, bells that ring spontaneously or musical instruments that seem to play on their own.

Among major cities, New York is especially rich with ghost stories. The spirit of Peter Stuyvesant, the city's last Dutch colonial governor, has been seen stomping around the East Village on his wooden leg since shortly after his death in 1672. The author Mark Twain is believed to haunt the stairwell of his onetime Village apartment building, while the ghost of poet Dylan Thomas is said to sometimes occupy his usual corner table at the West Village's White Horse Tavern, where he drank a fatal 18 shots of scotch in 1953. Perhaps the most famous New York ghost is that of Aaron Burr, who served as vice president under Thomas Jefferson but is best known for killing Alexander Hamilton in a duel in 1804. Burr's ghost is said to roam the streets of his old neighborhood (also the West Village). Burr's spectral ghost is said to roam the streets of his old neighborhood (also the West Village). Burr's spectral activity is focused particularly on one restaurant, One if By Land, Two if By Sea, which is located in a Barrow Street building that was once Burr's carriage house.

When I speak to people who believe in ghosts, I ask them why is a ghost dressed in clothes?

Aren't they supposed to be in spirit form?

Many times, their response is that, they never really thought about the clothes on the ghosts. Several agreed that it was a ridiculous notion to think that the clothes that the ghosts supposedly wore, stayed with them in the "afterlife."

The individuals who acknowledged the illogical idea that ghosts wear clothes, were also the ones that agreed that ghosts should not be able to make sounds without physical vocal cords.

One would have to create a new form of existence that goes against all of our physical laws.

The danger with that is, once you can make exceptions to the natural and physical laws of the universe, one can create anything, no matter how absurd it may be.

What people who believe in ghosts ought to think about is that, since the smart phones became part of our lives and 99.5% of all persons above the age of 10 has a cellphone, there have been almost NO pictures or videos of ghosts.

Strangely enough, before everyone had a cellphone, there were thousands of pictures of ghosts sent to newspapers all over the country.

In addition, many people have a program known as "Photoshop".

Photoshop allows one to manipulate picture and create pictures almost as if they were making a drawing or painting.

So, shouldn't it follow that there should have been many more photos of "ghosts" in the past few decades?

Well, there has not.

And one who does not suffer from Thinking Deficit Disorder should not have difficulty in determining the invalidity of pictures of ghosts.

Why did millions of people believe that Elvis Presley did not die?

He was a famous "early" rock and roll singer, songwriter, and guitar player.

He died at an early age of 42 from a severe heart attack.

He had an enlarged heart for a number of years and he also took many drugs, even though most of the drugs were mild.

Yet, millions of people throughout the world refused to accept that he died.

There were quite a number of "Elvis Sightings" around America and people believed that he faked his death because he was tired of all th fame and limelight and wanted to live on peace.

Over the years there have been countless alleged sightings – from right after Elvis' death up until the present day. Here's some of the most farfetched theories and Elvis spottings.

Shortly after Elvis' death, a man headed to Memphis airport and purchased a one-way ticket to Buenos Aires, Argentina. Reportedly the man looked like the pop star, and gave the name 'Jon Burrows' an alias of Elvis used when booking hotels for him; could it have actually been him?

In 'Home Alone'

There's a mad theory, discovered by <u>Noisey,</u> that points towards Elvis making an appearance in the 1990 film (so, 13 years after he died). As Kate checks flight availability, a bearded man is seen in the background – and the theory claims that the bearded fella is actually Elvis.

He looks around the right age (in 1990, Elvis would have been 55), there's some similarity in the eyes – and the hair colour is Elvis natural shade (he died his blond hair the trademark black). I mean, it's pretty tenuous, but stranger things have happened right? RIGHT?

In these cases, a clear and logical person can agree how powerful emotions are once again.

People's refusal to accept his death was purely emotional because they could not allow themselves to believe that such a charismatic person could die so suddenly.

Perhaps if he had cancer and died over a number of months, it may have allowed most of those "believers" to accept his death.

But to be alive one morning and die later that day, was too quick for the emotionally unstable people because they could not govern their emotions.

A major case for people who lack higher order thinking skills or have Thinking Deficit Disorder are those who believe in Alien Visitations.

The mythology began, in part, on the night of August 21, 1955, when a large extended farm family called the Suttons arrived breathlessly at the Hopkinsville police station in southwestern Kentucky. Their story of a terrifying siege by otherworldly beings would become one of the most detailed and baffling accounts of an alien close encounter on record—notable for the large number of witnesses nearly a dozen, the duration of the encounter several hours and the close proximity between the witnesses and creatures sometimes just a few feet away. The incident quickly became regional and even national news.

The alleged encounter occurred on the Suttons' farm in the tiny rural hamlet of Kelly, Kentucky, where the family lived in an unpainted three-room house without running water, telephone, radio, TV or books. Of all the details of their story—the UFO landing and the appearance of small alien creatures—one fact is indisputable: When the eight adults and three children arrived at the nearby Hopkinsville police station at about 11 p.m., they were genuinely terror-struck.

"These aren't the kind of people who normally run to the police for help," police chief Russell Greenwell later told investigators. "What they do is reach for their guns." Yet here they were, women and children hysterical and one man with a pulse of 140 beats per minute, measured by an investigator.

According to accounts given to the police, at about 7 p.m. on the hot Sunday evening, Sutton family friend Billy Ray Taylor was fetching water from the backyard well when he saw a silvery object, "real bright, with an exhaust all the colors of the rainbow." As he later recounted, it came silently toward the house, passed over it, stopped in the air—and then dropped straight to the ground.

Taylor, 21, and his 18-year-old wife had come from Pennsylvania to visit Lucky Sutton, with whom he had worked on a traveling carnival. The Suttons—50-year-old widow and matriarch Glennie Lankford, her two older sons and their wives, a brother-in-law and the widow's three younger children (12, 10, and 7)—didn't take Billy Ray seriously, laughing off his UFO account.

An hour later, alerted by the dog's incessant barking. Lucky and Billy Ray went to the back door and made out a strange glow, in the midst of which they spied a small humanoid creature. About three-and-a-half feet tall, it had an "oversized head…almost perfectly round, [its] arms extended almost to the ground, "Its" hands had talons…and [its oversized] eyes glowed with a yellowish light." The body gave off an eerie shimmer in the light of the night's new moon, they said—as if made of "silver metal."

Terrified, the two men grabbed a 20-gauge shotgun and a .22 rifle and fired at the "little man"—its "hands" now raised as if held up at gunpoint as it came toward the back door. They reported that it then did a "flip," scrambled upright and fled into the darkness.

Shortly after, the men saw a similar creature appear in a side window—and fired through the window screen. Still impervious to bullets, the "little man" again flipped, then disappeared. "I went out in the hallway and crouched down next to Billy, when I saw one approaching the door," Mrs. Lankford told Isabel Davis, author of an extensive report called "Close Encounter at Kelly and Others of 1955". "It looked like a five-gallon gasoline can with a head on top and small legs. It was a shimmering bright metal like on my refrigerator."

The drama escalated when Taylor stepped outside under the small overhanging roof, and those behind him saw a claw-like hand reach down and touch his hair. The group screamed and pulled Taylor back while Lucky shot above the overhang and then at another similar creature in a nearby tree. It floated to the ground and then scurried into the woods.

The Suttons moved inside and spent several hours listening for movements, hearing mostly occasional scratches on the roof. At 11 p.m., the whole group ran for the cars and high-tailed it to the Hopkinsville police station at top speed.

After the local police chief called for backup, his team was joined at the Sutton farm by state police, military police from nearby Fort Campbell and a photographer from the "The Kentucky New Era". There, investigators found shell casings from the gun shots, but no other evidence. Neither could they find proof of heavy drinking. According to the Sutton matriarch, "liquor was not allowed in the farmhouse."

Once the police and others left, though, the creatures returned between 2:30 a.m. and daybreak. Mrs. Lankford said she saw one glowing repeatedly by her bedside window, its claw-like hand on the screen.

The day after the incident, police investigators returned to the farmhouse, searching for evidence of a saucer landing, footprints, blood trails or scratch marks on the roof. They found nothing. Bud Ledwith, a local radio station employee, interviewed the adult eyewitnesses and made drawings based on their accounts. According to Davis,

he was impressed by their remarkable
specificity and consistency, even though
the men were away from the farmhouse
all day, unable to coordinate with the
others.

The story is quite compelling.

However, several things should stand
out.

First, the incredible lack of evidence
should immediately cause doubt among
a logical person.

Because logical thinkers, like scientists,
rely of facts.

When there are no facts, then evidence.

When no evidence, then indirect
evidence.

Then reasonable theory.

Then logical explanation

And finally, when all else fails, scientists and logical thinkers have what is called "probability."

In the case of the Sutters, they had no proof, no evidence, no logical explanation and not even probability.

So, a person with higher order thinking skills should determine that, either the family fabricated the story for several reasons or a combination of reasons, or, they did in fact see something and their own fears made them see aliens instead of something else.

What could that something else be?

Well, someone proposed that idea that the family had see two, Great Horned Owls.

They do have the same ears structure that the Sutters claimed they saw and those owls have large yellow, piercing and even, menacing looking eyes.

When their wings are down, they tend to hang all the way down to near its taloned feet.

If one sees photos of these Great Horned Owls and uses the higher thinking order skill of synthesis and some empathy, one will be able to understand how great fear from an ignorant person can see an alien out of an owl.

Think about all of the times people and even yourself, have heard a sound and imagined the worse.

And that sound grew more and more to what your mind was shaping it to be until you investigated and found out that the sound was not only made by something else, but it actually changed in noise once you understood what was making that sound.

The higher order thinking skill of synthesis can play the most important part in understanding the tremendously improbable chance of alien sightings.

Think about the fact that UFO sightings began to emerge all over the country as soon as a story came over the radio about a rancher who saw strange material on his farm.

The story grew into a phenomenon when one of the military men added to the story.

The famous story known as the Roswell incident became the catalyst to tens of thousands of "reports" of alien sightings.

Repots ranging from spaceships to actually, seeing the aliens became as

common as any other current event
story.

After all of the hysteria and stories about
the "Roswell Incident" reached abroad,
all of a sudden, reports of UFO sightings
began to emerge around the whole
world!

Coincidental or Thinking Deficit
Disorder?

Let's use logic and synthesis.

Whether or not you are good at math,
you can understand, compare and
contrast and have a fairly good idea of
the final numbers that I will present.

Have you ever picked up a handful of sand on the beach?

If you are one of the few who hasn't, perhaps you could imagine it.

Keep that in mind to understand the next, factual statement

There are more stars in the universe than all the grains of sand on every beach on this planet!

The number of stars in the universe is roughly 100 sextillion stars.

That number is too large for one to conceptualize in a meaningful way, so let us break that number down to one that is mor understandable.

If just 1% of all those stars had planetary systems around them, and then take 1% of that and assume that they are made of rock and then 1% of those have an electromagnetic field around them and then just 1% of those are in the right distance from their host star to have liquid water and then, just 1% of those planets do have liquid water and then just 1% of those worlds have simple cell or something simpler, bacteria. Then 1% of those planets evolved simple animals and then 1% of those worlds have complex animals, like cats and cows. And then, just 1% of those planets have civilizations and then 1% of those worlds have advanced civilizations.

Then, there would be at least 10 million planets with advanced civilizations.

That number is a logical, practical, and highly, probable number.

Finally, let us use a little imagination.

If a civilization found a way to travel faster than the speed of light or found some fantastic way to transport across stars and galaxies.

And we take 1% of those 10 million advanced civilizations, then one hundred thousand civilizations can space travel across tremendous distances.

That is how many stars there are in the universe. That is what more than 10 sextillion stars mean.

That is a pretty huge number, right?

Well, let us go back to the space traveling civilizations and think.

If one or more of those civilizations had the technology to travel to this planet from another solar system or another galaxy and did not want to be seen, how could one, actually believe that they saw an alien spacecraft, floating around our sky?

We, as a species have not been able to land people on another planet.

Only the moon.

Not even our nearest neighbor, Mars.

And we have the technology to hide our military aircraft not only out of visual range, but invisible to highly advanced radar systems.

Now use that logical synthesis,

How invisible would a much higher advanced species be to us?

So that is why I conclude that although it is possible and somewhat probable that we have been visited, I cannot think anything else but that if those aliens didn't want to be seen, then no one has ever saw an alien craft.

And if they did want to be seen, then they would land in Washington DC and say hello to the President.

Synthesis is very important to understand all of that which I had just proposed.

Think about this last example.

In the year 2021, Just One of our aircraft carrier attack groups can devastate and defeat the entire continent of Africa.

Yes, all 54 countries!

And as technologically inferior that Africa is to the United States, those present day, combined African countries could defeat the 1943 Germany.

The 1943 Germany military almost took over the world.

Just think about an alien race that is hundreds or thousands of years more advanced than us.

Then see how difficult it is to conclude that some random, farmer saw one floating around his barn.

I would like to end by leaving synthesis and higher order thinking for a moment and write about the enemy of logic.

That is, ungoverned emotions.

I found it quite amazing what this country went through with the previous administration.

I have followed politics since I was 14 years old and I have never witnessed such hatred for a president in my life.

What unsettled me the most was the reason for the hatred.

Millions of people hated President Trump before he started his first day in office.

I have not ever seen the media so blatantly opposed to president and worse, I have never witnessed such pure hatred of a president by the media.

Most of the media is democrat-liberal but they were always subtle in their bias.

From 2016-2020, I have seen the most shocking display of angry opposition to a president in my life.

False stories, exaggerated stories, and ridiculous accusations made up most of the news by the liberal media.

It was not only the cable news programs and the newspaper, but social media and other programs that used to try and remain neutral in the past.

I had to ask myself, what is all this hatred all about?

My conclusion was, once again, a combination of ungoverned emotions and Thinking Deficit Disorder.

October, 2016
Washington Post:

Whatever the outcome on Nov. 8, political uncertainty will follow: the months of transition, a change of White House staff, perhaps even the violent backlash that Trump may incite. This could be an excellent moment for a major Russian offensive: a land grab in Ukraine, a foray into the Baltic states, a much bigger intervention in the Middle East — anything to "test" the new president.

If that's coming, Putin needs to prepare his public to fight much bigger wars and to persuade the rest of the world not to stop him. He needs to get his generals into the right mind-set, and his soldiers ready to go. A little nuclear war rhetoric never fails to focus attention, and I'm sure it ha"The whole point of U.S. nuclear weapons control is to make sure that the president — and only the president — can use them if and whenever he decides to do so," Alex Wellerstein, the director of the science and technology studies program at the <u>Stevens Institute of Technology</u>, <u>wrote</u> in 2016 after Trump's election. "The one sure way to keep President Trump from launching a nuclear attack, under the system we've had in place since the early Cold War, would have been to elect someone else."

<u>No one can stop President Trump from using nuclear ...</u>
https://www.washingtonpost.com ›
2016/12/01 › no-on...

Dec 1, 2016 — The whole system is set up so the president — and only the president — can decide when to launch.

This book would have to be at least 4
thousand pages long in order to fit all of the
bias stories from the media.
And I would not even include all of the
hatred from social media,

So, again, I ask, where did all this hatred
come from?
What did this man do?

I have been aware for about twenty years;
how easily ignorant people can be
influenced to believe something.
But this case was extraordinary.

The following day after President Trump
was elected, a teacher threatened to throw
me down a flight of stairs because I stated
that I liked the fact that he won.
The teacher was not being humorous.
She was actually quite angry.
Why?
What did Trump do?

The media convinced millions of Americans that President Trump was going to destroy the economy.
The media said that Trump was a racist.
The media put out stories that Trump hated women.
Democrat officials said, on camera, that Trump was dangerous and could most likely trigger a series of events that would lead to a World War 3.
Based on what?

Well, this is what President Trump did to the economy:

- America gained 7 million new jobs – more than three times government experts' projections.

- Middle-Class family income increased nearly $6,000 – more than five times the gains during the entire previous administration.

- The unemployment rate reached 3.5 percent, the lowest in a half-century.

- Achieved 40 months in a row with more job openings than job-hirings.

- More Americans reported being employed than ever before – nearly 160 million.

- Jobless claims hit a nearly 50-year low.

- The number of people claiming unemployment insurance as a share of the population hit its lowest on record.

  Incomes rose in every single metro area in the United States for the first time in nearly 3 decades.

- Unemployment rates for African Americans, Hispanic Americans, Asian Americans, Native Americans, veterans, individuals with disabilities, and those without a high school diploma all reached record lows.

- Unemployment for women hit its lowest rate in nearly 70 years.

- Lifted nearly 7 million people off of food stamps.

- Poverty rates for African Americans and Hispanic Americans reached record lows.

- Income inequality fell for two straight years, and by the largest amount in over a decade.

- The bottom 50 percent of American households saw a 40 percent increase in net worth.

- Wages rose fastest for low-income and blue collar workers – a 16 percent pay increase.

- African American homeownership increased from 41.7 percent to 46.4 percent.

- The DOW closed above 20,000 for the first time in 2017 and topped 30,000 in 2020.

- The S&P 500 and NASDAQ have repeatedly notched record highs.

- Signed the Tax Cuts and Jobs Act – the largest tax reform package in history.

- More than 6 million American workers received wage increases, bonuses, and increased benefits thanks to the tax cuts.

- A typical family of four earning $75,000 received an income tax cut of more than $2,000 – slashing their tax bill in half.

- Doubled the standard deduction – making the first $24,000 earned by a married couple completely tax-free.

- Doubled the child tax credit.

- Immediately withdrew from the job-killing Trans-Pacific Partnership (TPP).

- Ended the North American Free Trade Agreement (NAFTA), and replaced it with the brand new United States-Mexico-Canada Agreement (USMCA).

- The USMCA contains powerful new protections for American manufacturers, auto-makers, farmers, dairy producers, and workers.

- The USMCA is expected to generate over $68 billion in economic activity and potentially create over 550,000 new jobs over ten years.

- Signed an executive order making it government policy to Buy American and Hire American, and took action to stop the outsourcing of jobs overseas.

- Negotiated with Japan to slash tariffs and open its market to $7 billion in American agricultural products and ended its ban on potatoes and lamb.

- Over 90 percent of American agricultural exports to Japan now receive preferential treatment, and most are duty-free.

- Negotiated another deal with Japan to boost $40 billion worth of digital trade.

- For the first time in nearly 70 years, the United States has become a net energy exporter.

- The United States is now the number one producer of oil and natural gas in the world.

- Natural gas production reached a record-high of 34.9 quads in 2019, following record high production in 2018 and in 2017.

- The United States has been a net natural gas exporter for three consecutive years and has an export capacity of nearly 10 billion cubic feet per day.

- Withdrew from the unfair, one-sided Paris Climate Agreement.

- Canceled the previous administration's Clean Power Plan, and replaced it with the new Affordable Clean Energy rule.

- Approved the Keystone XL and Dakota Access pipelines.

- Opened up the Arctic National Wildlife Refuge (ANWR) in Alaska to oil and gas leasing.

- Built over 400 miles of the world's most robust and advanced border wall.

- Illegal crossings have plummeted over 87 percent where the wall has been constructed.

- Deployed nearly 5,000 troops to the Southern border. In addition, Mexico deployed tens of thousands of their own soldiers and national guardsmen to secure their side of the US-Mexico border.

- Ended the dangerous practice of Catch-and-Release, which means that instead of aliens getting released into the United States pending future hearings never to be seen again, they are detained pending removal, and then ultimately returned to their home countries.

- Entered into three historic asylum cooperation agreements with Honduras, El Salvador, and Guatemala to stop asylum fraud and resettle illegal migrants in third-party nations pending their asylum applications.

- Withdrew from the horrible, one-sided Iran Nuclear Deal and imposed crippling sanctions on the Iranian Regime.

- Conducted vigorous enforcement on all sanctions to bring Iran's oil exports to zero and deny the regime its principal source of revenue.

- First president to meet with a leader of North Korea and the first sitting president to cross the demilitarized zone into North Korea.

- Maintained a maximum pressure campaign and enforced tough sanctions on North Korea while negotiating de-nuclearization, the release of American hostages, and the return of the remains of American heroes.

- Brokered economic normalization between Serbia and Kosovo, bolstering peace in the Balkans.

- Signed the Honk Kong Autonomy Act and ended the United States' preferential treatment with Hong Kong to hold China accountable for its infringement on the autonomy of Hong Kong.

- Recognized Jerusalem as the true capital of Israel and quickly moved the

American Embassy in Israel to Jerusalem.

- Acknowledged Israel's sovereignty over the Golan Heights and declared that Israeli settlements in the West Bank are not inconsistent with international law.

- Removed the United States from the United Nations Human Rights Council due to the group's blatant anti-Israel bias.

- Brokered historic peace agreements between Israel and Arab-Muslim countries, including the United Arab Emirates, the Kingdom of Bahrain, and Sudan.

- In addition, the United States negotiated a normalization agreement between Israel and Morocco, and recognized Moroccan Sovereignty over the entire Western Sahara, a position with long standing bipartisan support.

- Brokered a deal for Kosovo to normalize ties and establish diplomatic relations with Israel.

- Announced that Serbia would move its embassy in Israel to Jerusalem.

- First American president to address an assembly of leaders from more than 50 Muslim nations, and reach an agreement to fight terrorism in all its forms.

- Completely rebuilt the United States military with over $2.2 trillion in defense spending, including $738 billion for 2020.

- Secured three pay raises for our service members and their families, including the largest raise in a decade.

- Established the Space Force, the first new branch of the United States Armed Forces since 1947.

- Modernized and recapitalized our nuclear forces and missile defenses to ensure they continue to serve as a strong deterrent.

- Defeated 100 percent of ISIS' territorial caliphate in Iraq and Syria.

- Freed nearly 8 million civilians from ISIS' bloodthirsty control, and liberated Mosul, Raqqa, and the final ISIS foothold of Baghuz.

- Killed the leader of ISIS, Abu Bakr al-Baghdadi, and eliminated the world's top terrorist, Qasem Soleimani.

- Created the Terrorist Financing Targeting Center (TFTC) in partnership between the United States and its Gulf partners to combat extremist ideology and threats, and target terrorist financial networks, including over 60 terrorist individuals and entities spanning the globe.

- Twice took decisive military action against the Assad regime in Syria for the barbaric use of chemical weapons against innocent civilians, including a successful 59 Tomahawk cruise missiles strike.

- Signed and implemented the VA Mission Act, which made permanent Veterans CHOICE, revolutionized the VA community care system, and delivered quality care closer to home for Veterans.

- The number of Veterans who say they trust VA services has increased 19 percent to a record 91 percent, an all-time high.

- Offered same-day emergency mental health care at every VA medical facility, and secured $9.5 billion for mental health services in 2020.

- Signed the VA Choice and Quality Employment Act of 2017, which ensured that veterans could continue to see the doctor of their choice and wouldn't have to wait for care.

- Signed the bipartisan First Step Act into law, the first landmark criminal justice reform legislation ever passed to reduce recidivism and help former inmates successfully rejoin society.

- Promoted second chance hiring to give former inmates the opportunity to live crime-free lives and find meaningful employment.

- Launched a new "Ready to Work" initiative to help connect employers directly with former prisoners.

- In 2019, violent crime fell for the third consecutive year.

- Since 2016, the violent crime rate has declined over 5 percent and the murder rate has decreased by over 7 percent.

- Launched Operation Legend to combat a surge of violent crime in cities, resulting in more than 5,500 arrests.

- Deployed the National Guard and Federal law enforcement to Kenosha to stop violence and restore public safety.

- Provided $1 million to Kenosha law enforcement, nearly $4 million to support small businesses in Kenosha, and provided over $41 million to support law enforcement to the state of Wisconsin.

- Deployed Federal agents to save the courthouse in Portland from rioters.

- Signed an executive order outlining ten-year prison sentences for destroying Federal property and monuments.

- Moved the Federal Historically Black Colleges and Universities (HBCU) Initiative back to the White House.

- Signed into law the FUTURE Act, making permanent $255 million in annual funding for HBCUs and increasing funding for the Federal Pell Grant program.

- Signed legislation that included more than $100 million for scholarships, research, and centers of excellence at HBCU land-grant institutions.

- Fully forgave $322 million in disaster loans to four HBCUs in 2018, so they could fully focus on educating their students.

What can an objective and logical person conclude?

That President created the second-best economy in U.S. history.

He did more for African Americans than anyone except President Lincoln and President Kennedy.

President Trump won THREE Nobel Peace Prize nominations, that is more than any president in U.S. history.

To any logical person, President Trump did the opposite of what the media predicted he would do.

But there is still a missing component.

Where did all that hatred come from.

Predicting that a president was going to do a bad job and being wrong about it is one thing.

Having utter contempt for Trump is something else.

Where did all that hatred come from?

Surely the media played the largest part, but why?

One could only conclude that it was the way President Trump spoke.

But, I, like so many people believe that Actions Speak Louder Than Words.

It is apparent that most people do not believe that phrase.

Their emotions prevented them from seeing the President clearly, honestly, and objectively.

I will not discuss what occurred in the 2020 election and how four states changed rules and how Covid 19 indirectly allowed for corruption in the voting system by resulting in mail in ballot voting.

I will let history judge what happened.

But I would like to conclude by stating that ungoverned emotions and Thinking Deficit Disorder can have devastating consequences.

Perhaps, one day, I hope someone, if not me, can and will do something very difficult.

That is, to create a "How To" book on using higher order thinking skills and governing one's emotions.

My final political message to All Americans is….

Treat your country the way you treat your home.

The Chosen #13

Rob's cousins Ed and Clyde and Ed's family all rushed to the spaceship, Zephyr.

Ed was the last one to be rescued from the small house.

Just as Jack was about to board the space craft, he heard a strange noise.

Rapidly turning his head, he saw a raged human running toward the spacecraft.

He aimed his alien rifle at the individual.

Rob witnessed Jack's action and called out to him.

"Don't shoot!" He shouted. "That thing is far enough."

Jack quickly agreed with Rob and simply jumped into the spaceship.

Rob closed the sliding door screen.

It caused the three-step case to fold in an instant followed by the doors sliding shut.

"Buckle in, everyone!" Rob ordered as he shut all the windows closed with a shielding plate that slid down over them.

All it took was a one second swipe of a panel screen.

He didn't want the children to see this wild person, who just reached the ship.

The male, raged human began to bang and pound the exterior of the the Zephyr.

"Are you ready, Jack?" Rob asked, giving him a quick glance.

"Yes." His best friend replied as he strapped on the seating harness.

Rob slid two of his fingers over a longer panel screen and the space vessel began to turn around.

"Okay everyone, we are going to launch now!" Rob called to the people on the ship.

Suddenly the ship, ignoring the crazed person who was hitting it, raced down the desolate street and lifted into the air two seconds later.

Once in the air, Rob touched the small panel which lifted all of the window screens.

As the usual response, Rob's cousins were dumbfounded by what they were experiencing.

Books by Decabo

Of the Lake

Communed

Rukoya

Green Hearts

Rukoya and the Razorek
Coven

Diemond Seek

Over Procyon

Periwinkle Snow

Samhain

Open This Can

Those among Them

What do You Think
About?

Cycle of Fright

Strange Favors

Our Gathering

Invasion of Anbell

Journals from Mars

My sister, Jetta

Philip's Last Night

Think a Little

Rukoya short story series

Angry Witness

Hiding

Razorek

Coercion

The Coven

Resurfaced

Blood Family

Rejection

Mitchell Four

Deadly Scarecrow

Union

The Preserved

Ancient Ones

Terror of Spring Heeled Jack

Queen Argenta

Mrs. Avid

Fury of the Moon Witch

Phantom Coach

Nimbus

Fusion of the Lake

The Wise Girls short story series

#1

#2 The Chosen starts

#3

#4

#5

#6

#7

#8

#9

#10

#11

#12

#13